Dr. Michal Schanin & Vera Yogev

Between the Lines

Developing Strategic Reading Skills
Instruction | Learning | Alternative Assessment

Workbook 1

Senior Editors & Producers: Contento
Translation: Naama Meron-Asher
Editing: Gayla Goodman
Book Design: Liliya Lev Ari

Copyright © 2016 by Dr. Michal Schanin & Vera Yogev and Contento

All rights reserved. No part of this book may be translated, reproduced, stored in a retrieval system or transmitted, in any form or by any means, electronic, photocopying, recording or otherwise, without prior permission in writing from the author and publisher.

ISBN: 978-965-550-515-3

International sole distributor: Contento
22 Isserles Street, 6701457 Tel Aviv, Israel

www.ContentoNow.com
Netanel@contento-publishing.com

Dr. Michal Schanin & Vera Yogev

Between the Lines

Developing Strategic Reading Skills
Instruction | Learning | Alternative Assessment

Workbook 1

Table of Contents

Introduction 7

   1. The Tortoise and the Hare 29

   2. "Why Are the Leaves of the Tree Blue?" 46

   3. Why Does the Ox Walk Slowly? 59

   4. A Nice Tale that Happened in our Town 65

   5. The Sweetest Music in the World 77

   6. Keep an Eye on the Door 91

Assessment Tools 101

   1. Alternative Assessment — Indicator of Reading and Comprehension on Three Levels of Thinking 101

   2. Learning Journal 105

Tables of Graded Language Patterns 111

Table of Workbook 1 Texts and Skills 116

Introduction

When one delves into the professional literature about reading, one might come across many publications on this subject. However these articles might not offer a satisfying explanation about the process of acquiring reading.

In the past, a common and prevailing belief maintained that if students were to be confronted with questions about the content of the text, eventually they would understand its meaning independently. Yet today it is widely accepted that the extent and depth of reading processes are not as simple as that.

The process of extracting meaning out of texts encompasses various aspects. Take, for example, producing meaning out of the text and augmenting, assessing and creating new meanings out of this text. It turns out that acquiring the meaning of a text is not restricted only to processing information, finding answers and the automatic output of deciphering text. In contrast, acquiring the meaning of a text is a complex multi-dimensional process.

Every reader can achieve and develop a process of producing meaning from the text, and in this way exercise beneficial skills and strategies that help understand the meaning. Therefore, teachers should instruct their students in ways to pair skills and strategies to various reading situations while relying on syntactic, semantic and pragmatic clues in order to extract meaning from a text.

The development of reading and the production of meaning from a text happen simultaneously to many other interrelated skills. Readers often find that their involvement in the reading process and in the grapho-phonemic deciphering process assists their capability to understand the context. These skills guide children through the deciphering process. Simultaneously, it provides them with feedback as to the extent of correctness achieved by their deciphering.

Reading is an interactive process that interrelates many varied skills. To achieve skilled reading, one must develop reading skills and strategies that may avail one during reading. Integral integration of the whole pack of strategies—deciphering and understanding while applying meta-cognitive checking—can lead readers to skilled reading. These reading skills serve as a toolbox for the readers and help them with reading and understanding texts. Skillful readers transform skills into an integral part of the process of reading. Thus for example, readers can understand the main idea of a text quickly and precisely, foretell coming events in the text, draw conclusions from a text and apply the meaning of the text to their own personal lives.

The skill of producing meaning from a text might become an automatic and unaware one, but using strategies is a result of a well-informed and intentional discretion: how to cope with reading tasks and which skills to use.

Pearson et al. (1990) emphasized in their research that not only the reader's skills but also the right timing is necessary. Both capabilities–the ability to plan reading and the right timing–create a productive result in achieving reading strategies and meta-cognitive control.

We have learned from our long-term work in the educational field that teachers need to put theoretical methods into practice. These skills and strategies are highly important in developing language education in the various populations of students.

We have chosen from the varied curriculum of language education a genre (system) that can demonstrate to teachers and students some core strategies. After becoming familiar with them, they can put them into practice.

Basic Hypotheses

* Language education takes on language both as a means and an end in developing students' language efficiency in oral and written language.

* Preschool children start their schooling geared with a wide and varied linguistic knowledge (mainly their proficiency of oral language) but also of written language. This knowledge is expressed through understanding and production of clauses and phrases and through the unique meanings a child may attach to them.

* One can detect a variance in the level of language acquisition among peers. This variance is manifested through the pace of acquiring reading, vocabulary, discourse styles, cognitive development and more.

* Written language can be challenging for the acquiring student; direction and explicit learning in class is needed to help him or her with this.

* The notion *language* refers to various communication channels and to different discourse styles as well as to varied levels of language and genres.
* The genre that was selected for this book specifically refers to folktales, fables and folklore.
* Knowledge of language may include both grammatical and practical proficiency and the know-how of using language in different contexts.
* The knowledge of language is acquired through textual contexts.
* By initially practicing patterns that consist of simple phrases in order to gradually acquire a language, the learner progresses to building up more complex sentences that he or she can grasp with the mind.

Aims of Language Education

A meta-aim of language education is to foster a literate person for whom language can meet with the reader's communicative needs:

* Producing meaning from written texts and maintaining a well-informed use of the unique genre we chose for this book.
* Providing tools and skills that deliver knowledge about language and learning strategies that will be acquired by using this specific genre and applying these tools, skills and strategies to other genres.
* Developing an informed reading ability of literary texts and Jewish folktales and maintaining a dialogue with Jewish sources.
* Developing students' capability of written expression, which allows them to express their inner and outer worlds.
* Learning the various usages of language: listening, speaking, reading and writing. These usages interrelate with skills that are involved with understanding and expressing language.
* Developing activities that foster meta-linguistic knowledge about language (learning journal, indicators).

* Developing the ability to pass on knowledge through speech, writing and reading exercises.
* Handling texts while manipulating a structured learning of linguistic patterns (language patterns) in order to gear learners with various tools that allow self-expression, reading comprehension and critical, analytical and evaluation reading.

The Goals of Language Education

* Development of skills and strategies that structure the meaning of the text while providing a toolbox that can help students through the reading process.
* Development of thinking skills in students through reading that spans from a verbal production of meaning to providing an applied meaning of a text.
* Development of language enrichment for students by gradually providing them with linguistic tools that can present them with the basics of meaningful reading.
* Development of retrieving and matching capabilities in students that enable them to match various strategies and skills to varied types of texts.
* Development of capabilities in students to transform various strategies and apply them correctly in all types of texts in Hebrew learning environments such as history, Bible, geography, etc.
* Development of appreciation and control processes in students, which are based on indicators. These indicators are a part of the criteria that belong to each strategy.
* Development of reflection and feedback in students about all processes of learning, thinking, and reading while using a learning journal that documents their reading.
* Enhancing teachers' capabilities of mediating between text and reader. At the same time, adjusting skills and reading strategies that facilitate a meaningful understanding of the text.
* Enhancing the teacher's skill of establishing various independent tasks at different thought levels, following the example molded by this workbook.

* Enhancing the teacher's awareness of the *passages,* scaling up from literate to interpretive understanding. Directing a teacher's attention to differences that might exist among the students in the class.

Principles of the Program

The program focuses on the control of managing literacy in discourse, which enables speakers to adjust their language to social circumstances and aims, to various knowledge areas and to their previous knowledge of a target population. The language education curriculum aims to cover various texts that belong to genres and sub-genres of varied fields of knowledge. Literacy functioning is the ability to understand different genres and use them in oral conversation. In this program we chose one genre in particular. We formulated six texts for each age group. Our program deals with the full literate discourse that is very characteristic of tales, fables and folktales. Being part of the curriculum, this choice intends to meet with two of our aims: first to practice language and then to help with the production of meaning from texts. Students love and are willing to use this genre, and they find it fun and motivating personally and culturally. Our second aim is to enable students to learn a lesson from this genre. The program enhances the student's listening and oral expression skills. We also made sure to integrate these skills in various activities. The skill of developing listening abilities is an outcome of a constant dialogue that exists between the spoken and written discourses.

During the program, students are asked to listen to the teacher or their peers who read to them in front of the whole class. The workbook assignments are latterly practiced in groups or individually and at the end of the activity each group or individual presents their thoughts to the whole class

The feedback—a learning journal will document their learning, enabling the students to follow up on the meta-cognitive processes.

By using these meta-cognitive processes, students may acquire both linguistic knowledge and may understand various genres and subgenres of texts.

The World of Discourse—The Genre: Legends, Tales and Fables

Legends, tales and fables all belong to one genre that provides insights into past or present events together with an added value of their cultural and authentic facets. The strict and set structure of this genre is based on its background, its characters and its lessons to be learned. In order to learn how to forge meaning out of these characteristics, learners are provided with strategies that reflect and focus on differences that exist in this genre and point to variances that can be found in the backgrounds, structures, messages, characters and their interactions with our tales.

The most prominent characteristic of this genre is its formal construction, which consists of introduction, setting, conflict, catharsis or peak, resolution, turning point and conclusion.

In order to understand the process in texts, an awareness must be raised in students to the sequence of the plot, its details and the characters. Students learn how to separate the wheat from the chaff, both orally and textually. To acquire these strategies students are dependent on their linguistic knowledge of verbs, adjectives, structural words and phrases, which altogether are very helpful in delivering the entire plot and subtexts.

Through reading the text, readers can establish their own personal interpretations and crystallize their attitudes to it; allowing them to make their own premises and draw conclusions that result in a critical reading of the text. All these traits are immensely helpful and ameliorate students' understanding of the text and help develop various skills.

In addition, readers format their own personal viewpoint of the text and can identify with the author's viewpoint.

Leading the learner to these outcomes should happen through practicing various and relevant learning strategies. At the same time learners must use appropriate language structures.

About the Program

Based on a cognitive approach, the underlying features of our program *Between the Lines* include using reading skills and strategies as well as harnessing the student's meta-cognitive system for directing and orienting reading (Pearson 1990).

According to this approach there are seven principle characteristics that are shared by all skilled readers without regard to their level or age:

1. A reader can easily separate the wheat from the chaff.
2. Readers look for a link between material they know and newly read material.
3. A reader establishes a hypothetical model for the newly read themes; a model to be tested throughout reading.
4. The model established by the reader will be remodeled according to conclusions the reader draws from the meaning of the text.
5. A reader can summarize what she or he has just read.
6. A reader is efficient in drawing conclusions throughout and after the process of reading and can achieve full understanding of the text.
7. A reader can independently raise questions about the author, the text and themselves.

All these skills should be acquired by readers so they can potentially reach a better understanding of the text.

The *Between the Lines* program applies to three levels of thinking:
1. A literal understanding of the text.
2. An interpretative level of the text.
3. An implemental level of the text.

After being divided into sub-skills, these levels can be found helpful in creating intermediate stages in the process of reading and producing the text meaning. We developed our method through eclectic and integrative means and "implementation tools;" namely the above-mentioned skills and strategies that interweave through the three levels of understandings mentioned above. These implementation tools should meet with most of the needs of our student populations, including under-achieving populations and special-needs students. Our program has put an emphasis on linguistic enrichment and practice while paying attention to the deep structural layers of language and linguistic enrichment. This emphasis is manifested through the following implementation tools:

* Graded linguistic patterns.

* Implicit and explicit content clues.
* General and linguistic cloze excerpts.

The graded linguistic patterns are syntactical structures that provide the entire components of the English language.

Implicit and explicit content clues—provide accessories for the reader. Through locating these implicit and explicit content clues a student becomes an independent, skilled and efficient reader. The content clues allow him or her to unfold meaning and internal contexts of a sentence.

Cloze passages—texts that have blanks in them where some of the words in the texts are missing. By recovering the excerpt through embedding the omitted words, a student can test his or her proficiency by using the three above-mentioned levels of text understanding.

In order to be able to recover a deficient passage the student should command these skills: linguistic skills, the ability of contextual and textual repetition and pragmatic and cultural knowledge skills.

* Linguistic skills—includes vocabulary and syntax.
* Contextual ability—the links that tie together parts of a text .
* Pragmatic knowledge—former knowledge that can be applied.
* Cultural knowledge—a culture-dependent knowledge.

Our *Between the Lines* program integrates both tools of assessment and measuring that yield feedback and reflection to teachers about their methods of teaching, about their students' learning and student-teacher interrelated dialogue.

The two assessment tools that were selected for *Between the Lines* are:
1. Learning journal
2. Indicators

Both tools help to develop teacher-learner communication. They also contribute to formative assessment and summative assessment.

1. Learning Journal

A learning journal is one of the learning and assessment tools designed for acquiring knowledge through the raising of guided questions. It prompts the intrinsic self-searching of students and encourages them to look closely at their learning processes.

A learning journal can store all the linkages and products that were documented by learners throughout their learning processes. It offers an initial stock of learning processes.

By verbalizing their thinking processes, learners can raise awareness of their learning experiences. Journals can also provide them with fresh knowledge about their own learning and thinking strategies (Birnbaum, 1999). Learners can also retrospectively view their successes and challenges. Furthermore, verbalizing of thinking processes can help students enhance their potential for being "independent learners."

The components of our Learning Journal include:

* Addressing the gist of knowledge.
* Addressing and locating challenges.
* Finding a link between prior personal knowledge and current knowledge.
* Forming an opinion and taking a stand.

2. Indicators

An Indicator is based on yardsticks that familiarize students with what is expected of them throughout the upcoming assignments.

Each indicator manifests some dimensions, which are needed for giving indication about the quality of students' work. They can usually be further divided into three levels of student control and performance:

* At the beginning—students are without control.
* On their way to goal-achieving—are partly in control.
* Fully achieving their goal—are in full control.

The characteristics of these yardsticks apply to each of the above-mentioned levels of performance. By tracing these characteristics, teachers and students can diagnose the level of performance achieved and what should be improved and/or strengthened. In the same vein, these characteristics can point to weaknesses and strengths of the learning process.

The Indicator is a guiding light that students follow on their way to achieving their goals—control and strategy. These yardsticks present the students, in painstaking detail, the expectations of their performance. Success measures can mirror students' abilities and direct them to achieving higher levels of success.

By being a teacher-student interactive tool, the Indicator helps teachers continue to be persistent and accurate in their evaluations. By enabling students to realize their own challenges and strengths, the Indicator also raises awareness of their teacher's expectations and evaluations.

Design of the Program

This program is comprised of three workbooks that were especially designed for enhancing reading and thinking and for acquiring text meaning by way of implementing tools for self-evaluation and measuring for learners and teachers.

Aimed at 2nd to 6th graders and their teachers, the program can be modularly implemented by the teacher by matching the level of workbook to his or her class level, in full accord with students' needs.

The program allows teachers to choose and delegate various assignments to different students. Its underlying objective is to develop appropriate reading and writing skills in students that are needed for a versed usage of the written language.

By not aiming at specific student knowledge that was learned in class and by not testing it, the program alternatively provides students with skills they need for functional literacy. It also supports them in learning which skills and thinking strategies are needed for each specific literacy activity.

Each workbook contains a repository of six literary texts that were extracted from a widely-accepted curriculum for elementary schools. In each text, the three levels of thinking (verbal understanding, interpretive understanding and the implemental level) are practiced. There are sub-skills in each level of thinking that are also practiced, and all in all they are aimed at developing a meta-cognitive thinking ability that provides guidance for using the right tools. Each workbook contains an introduction that was written for teachers and parents, illuminating the principles and goals of the program.

Verbal Understanding

The level of verbal understanding includes the following skills:

Sequence

The narrative sequence is practiced in the current workbook through using:

1. A sequence of segments.
2. A sequence of key sentences.
3. A sequence of keywords.
4. A sequence of questions.

Workbook 1 places a special emphasis on the issue of sequential abilities. Sequence in narratives is a topic that has been thoroughly investigated in literature. It was found that when students achieve an understanding of the narrative sequence of a text they can also grasp more than 50 percent of the text content without dwelling on minute narrative details.

B. The Skill of Finding Detail

The skill of finding detail is practiced in this workbook by raising questions such as:

1. Who said this to whom?
2. Find an alternative word.
3. True or False?
4. Classification tables.

A reader can piece together the details of the narrative sequence by using this skill.

C. Locating a Main Idea

Locating a main idea is practiced in this workbook by locating a key sentence of the text that holds a wealth of keywords. Linking keywords by conjunctions will lead readers to the sentence that presents the main idea of the text.

D. Raising and Classifying Questions

Being a meta-cognitive skill, this ability is practiced in the workbook by using interrogatives, namely WH-words, in readers' three levels of thinking:

Literal level of questions	Interpretive level of questions	Implemental questions
Who?	Why?	What did you feel…?
What?	How?	What do you think…?
How much?	Whether?	What would you do instead…?
Where to?	Which?	Was the author right when…?
Where?	How come?	Why do you think it happened….?
Where?	In which way?	What would you do if…?

The practice of raising questions in these three levels of thinking and at the same time compiling them and classifying them in tables, supports the development of thinking in students.

E. Mapping out of Concepts

To exercise this skill we developed three tools for knowledge management. The beneficial aspect of these tools is that they allow for plotting graphical maps out of linear text. Using keywords and conjunctions and embedding them in these maps helps the student sum up the text.

The three tools of knowledge management are:

1. Flow charts.
2. Venn Diagrams.
3. Diffuse Mapping.

1. Flow Charts

Flow charts are helpful in tracking plots and sequences of events or can be used in scientific texts that are based on cause and effect.

By plotting a chart, a learner defends his or her understanding of the text. By embedding keywords and key sentences in a chart a learner manifests his or her ability to separate the wheat from the chaff.

Flow charts can also be utilized for developing the skill of summarization. This skill consists of using keywords and key sentences and of integrating conjunctions to make a link between them.

2. Venn Diagrams

This tool can be used in cases when we want to demonstrate contrast and to compare things (intersection and union). Embedding keywords and key sentences in these diagrams trains learners to separate the wheat from the chaff.

For example:

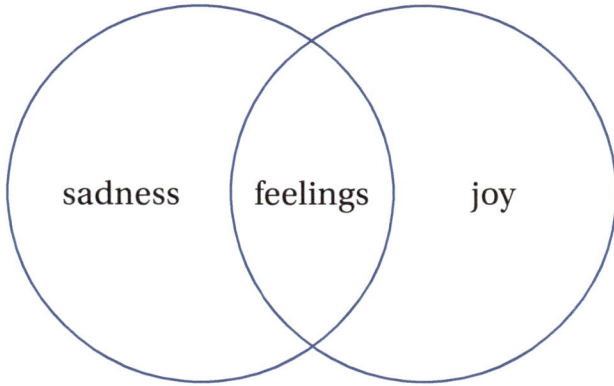

Through using Venn Diagrams, one can develop his or her summarization skills: joining together keywords and key sentences within the Venn diagram and then making a connection between them with a conjunction and creating a summarization out of them.

3. Concept Map

Using this mapping helps students to select factual information from informative texts, if the sequential order is irrelevant in these texts.

To organize this factual information a student can plot it in classification tablets that consist of columns of generalizing semantic categories. In this way items are grouped together under the same category. This tool for organizing information is selected according to the text genre.

F. Classification

This ability is practiced through using classification tables in the current workbook. Classification tables are information organizers. They are built by manipulating either inductive or deductive reasoning. In more simple words, the method of reasoning can derive general principles from particular facts or derive the reasoning by going from the general to the specific facts.

G. Separating the Wheat from the Chaff

To encourage students to practice this skill, the workbook offers three principle tools:

1. Naming the sequence of segments.
2. Locating key sentences.
3. Locating keywords.

1. Naming the Sequence of Segments

The skill of naming the sequence of segments entails one to locate the meaningful segments of the narrative, to identify bridging passages between segments and to give titles for each segment separately. The resulting sequence of titles will yield a synopsis of the narrative.

2. Locating Key Sentences

The text key sentences are those that are most significant in each segment; sentences that without them a segment would be meaningless.

There are two main questions for locating and identifying key sentences in each segment.

a. Who is the segment talking about?

b. What is the segment talking about?

The answers to these questions might be either one or several key sentences of a text.

3. Locating Keywords

The text keywords are the main words in the sentence that if omitted in the sentence might cause the sentence to become meaningless. In order to locate keywords in a sentence we need to ask two questions:

a. Who is the sentence talking about?

b. What is the sentence talking about?

H. Linguistic Program

The linguistic-syntactic enrichment of our program is an integral part that integrates graded linguistic structures in most stories. We built up the linguistic training through various tools beginning from simple linguistic-syntactic patterns through to complex syntactical structures:

1. Graded linguistic patterns.
2. Cloze.
3. Explicit and implicit content clues.

1. Graded linguistic patterns

Linguistic patterns are a sequence of syntactic structures that are gradually built up and accumulated: from simple to compound and complex sentences.

These syntactical structures are organized and graded according to a sequential development of language (see a continuum of linguistic patterns achieved at the end of workbook).

2. Cloze

A cloze is based on the meaning of the whole story but certain words are omitted from the text and the blanks create deficiencies in the integrity of the text.

This exercise allows readers to conjecture about the missing words and base their conjectures on the context of the text and by the way they understand its meaning. This ability can be achieved via three skills:

* Linguistic skill

- * Context and textual repetition
- * Linguistic skill + textual repetition and context + pragmatic knowledge

Linguistic skills—the ability to reconcile deficient text by repairing it with vocabulary from former linguistic and syntactic repertoire.

Context and textual repetition—the ability to pick out a word from the text and repeat it in the right context in order to reconcile the deficient text.

Linguistic ability + context and textual repetition + pragmatic knowledge—allows for recalling of former knowledge (cultural, linguistic and pragmatic knowledge) and thus it facilitates in completing a deficient sentence.

I. Explicit and Implicit Content Clues

The linguistic ability of locating implicit and explicit content clues helps learners to independently highlight meanings from the text and to become independent and skilled readers without becoming dependent on dictionaries and teachers. See the flow chart on the next page.

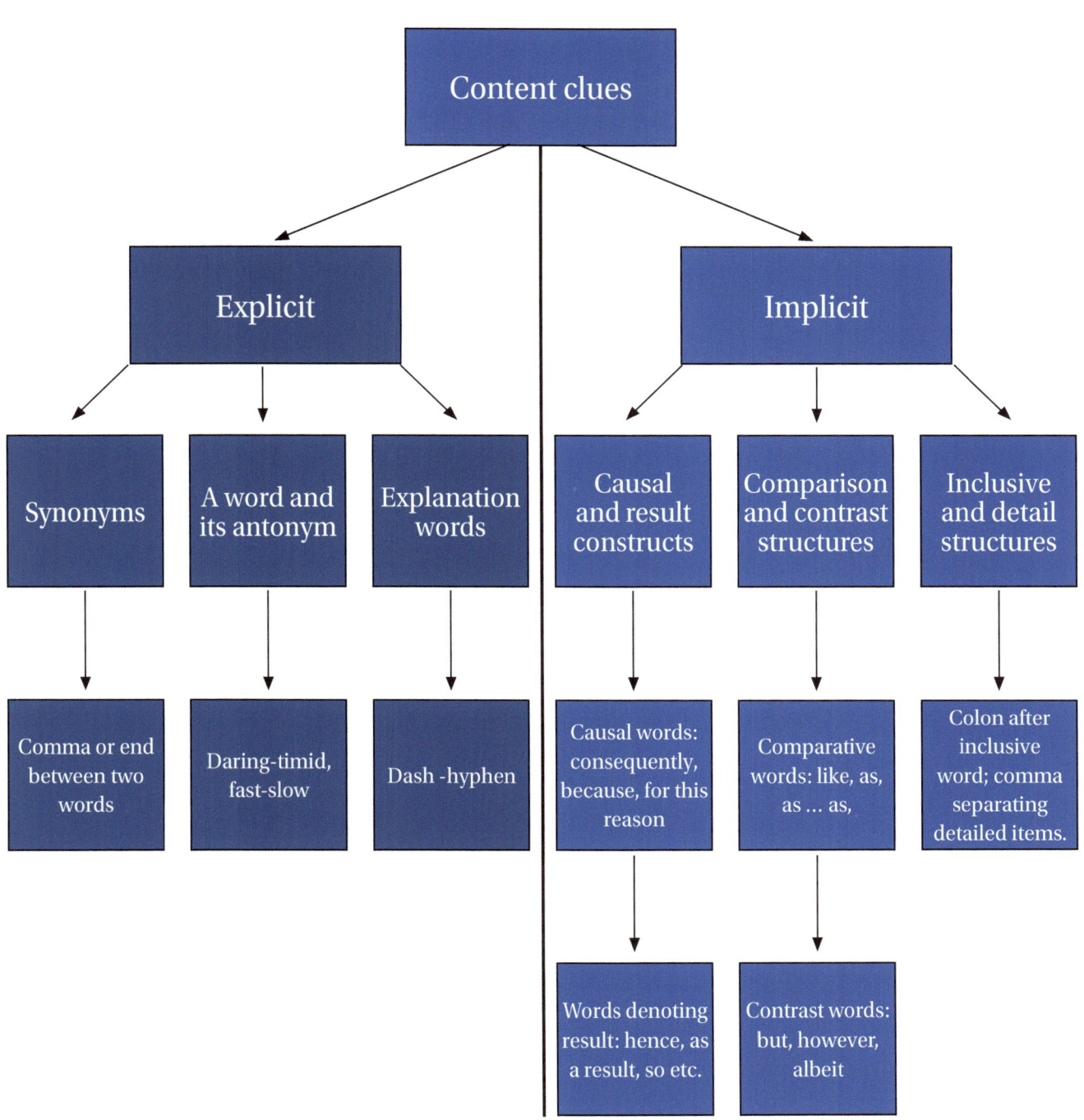

An Implicit Level of Interpretation

a. **Foretelling of Events**—this skill offers a reader the practice of reading between the lines. The reading goes beyond the written text and projects and foretells what will come next. By basing one's projections on logical thinking, this skill suggests a type of reading that will actively search for objectives while reading and will lead learners to establish some hypotheses about the text and then to test them.

Although this skill can lead to the establishment of some correct hypotheses, the result will be prescribed by the information of the text.

b. **Locating an Implicit Unstated Main Idea of a Text**—this skill develops in a reader the expertise of finding an idea not stated that can be traced by reading between the lines; namely by reading the text and locating the main ideas that are either predictable or interpretable.

First and foremost this skill is based on finding the main idea of a text while using an immediate verbal understanding.

Next a reader is called upon to render an interpretation and give some thought in order to locate an unstated main idea.

c. **Drawing Conclusions**—the skill of drawing conclusions is an outcome of the implicit unstated main idea of a text. To achieve this skill a reader must render inductive and deductive thinking that can lead them to draw conclusions. Next, by basing the accumulation of interpreted sentences of a text, a reader can "justify" or reason the conclusions that were reached about the text.

d. **Identifying the Author's Viewpoint**—by using this skill a student identifies an author's personal implied viewpoint and/or attitude, when it is not explicitly stated in the text.

This skill is achievable through instructing a reader to look for clues that would showcase an author's viewpoint and ground them by citing phrases from the text.

e. **Reading the Protagonist's Feelings and Analyzing Characters**—this skill is achievable by developing a reader's sensitivity to be able to pinpoint a character or protagonist's personal feelings and characteristics and by instructing them to base their insights on the traceable physical portrayal and responses of characters.

Furthermore, classifying sentence tables that portray each character, a tool that was formerly demonstrated in a more primordial verbal comprehension phase, can also be found to be helpful for portraying characters.

f. **Linguistic Enrichment**—this skill consists of three above-mentioned linguistic enrichment tools and the building up of graded language. It is part and parcel of the literary subject that is simultaneously being taught.

Implemental Phase

In this phase a learner finally integrates skills that were acquired through the verbal and interpretive reading levels. In the implemental phase, the student can begin to link problem solving and implementation from within texts to application of these skills in real life situations.

Another skill suggested by this phase is critical reading of texts and assessing their correctness. Critical reading of a text is not achievable until a reader has used his or her verbal and interpretive reading skills for comprehending the author's main ideas. By doing so they can answer questions, a skill that is based on abstract thinking. However, in many cases the text offers some equally probable and acceptable answers to a specific question. The implementation level consists of the following skills:

a. **Problem Solving**

This skill is developed when reading material is the source for problem solving abilities eventually applied to the problems of daily life. This skill is equally accessible for any age of the reader. An equally important fact is that for each problem there are several equally acceptable solutions.

b. Critical Reading

Critical reading of a text is a more advanced cognitive skill than the implemental level or critical thinking. It involves the assessment and judgment of the text based on either a reader's own experience or on learned information.

While using the skill of critical reading a reader assesses the level of persuasiveness of a text at three different levels:

1. The level of its accuracy.
2. Distinguishing between opinions and facts.
3. Identifying literary/ literariness material.

Level of Text Accuracy

This skill involves exercising judgment and assessment over the level of literary or scientific accuracy of material learned by the student. This entails pointing out inaccuracies, stale or provocative facts, or out-of-date, inaccurate or irrelevant content.

Distinguishing Between Opinions and Facts

This skill involves the ability to distinguish between opinions and facts of a text, which is quite a complicated skill because sometimes opinions and facts are inseparably interwoven. Thus a reader might learn that a fact based on a valid fact is stronger than a baseless opinion.

Identifying Literary Material

This skill can help students distinguish between various literary genres e.g. prose, folktales, fables, scientific papers, propaganda etc. and to identify provocative sentences and announcements that are intended to persuade and make people change their minds, namely political articles. This is how students may learn about different methods of propaganda.

In Conclusion

The *Between the Lines* program practices the three levels of text understanding: its verbal, interpretive and implementation levels while foregrounding its linguistic program as an inseparable part of them. Some of the program texts exercise all three levels of thinking and skills. Others may only partially apply manipulate the set of understanding levels and skills. Hence, teachers are advised to add more skills to this triad of understanding levels and to use more skills that match their class level and fit variances among the students. The workbook icons:

 Verbal Understanding  Linguistic Understanding

 Interpretative Understanding  Implementation

 An explanation for students about the workbook's various learning skills.

 An explanation for both teachers and students about the workbook's various activities: oral and writing skills, listening, acting, painting and comics.

The Tortoise and the Hare
by Aesop

Light-footed is the hare, quick-witted is the tortoise.

One day the nimble hare said to the plodding tortoise, "Let's have a race. The one that finishes first will win the victory cup."

Surely enough, he was convinced that no one could beat him, because he was the swiftest of runners, everybody knew that.

"Okay," said the tortoise. "I accept your challenge; we shall see who has the last laugh. There, at the end of the road, is the finish line!"

The race began to the sound of a whistle blown by a dwarf. The tortoise plodded slowly to the starting point.

The hare, brimming with self-confidence, did not even bother to step up to the starting point. Instead he leaned back on the roadside and taunted the tortoise, "Move it kiddo, move it!"

The tortoise did not pay attention and plodded heavily forward, which made the hare even more scornful and laugh even harder. The tortoise was laboriously plodding along while the hare yelled at him, "When I hit the road, I'll make the dust fly! Hurry up, otherwise it will take the whole night to end this thing."

"That's alright with me, don't move a muscle, hare," the tortoise breathed heavily, and made his way slowly but confidently. "You can say what you please, but I'm going to leave you in the dust. We shall see who the winner will be!"

"You, beat me?! Ha, that's hilarious! What nonsense! Who ever heard of a tortoise that can outrun a hare? I can take you over however I want and in any event I will!"

The tortoise heard that, kept his mouth shut, and laboriously continued ploddingly away.

"The poor thing has not even made it half way. Meanwhile I will take a little nap, because I can always beat him," muttered the hare and lay down to sleep.

While the hare was napping, his snoring sounded like sneering, jeering at the efforts of the tortoise.

When the hare opened his eyes, what did he see? The tortoise had almost reached the finish line; only a little step separated him from it.

Leaping up high, as fast as the wind, the hare started to sprint, but all for nothing, he was too late. The tortoise took one little step further. He reached the finish line first and won the victory cup.

"You see," concluded the tortoise. "Next time, dear friend, don't waste words; actions speak louder than words."

Verbal Understanding

A. Development of Sequential Abilities

The following paragraphs are not in the correct order. Rearrange them in the correct order by giving each paragraph a number.

> **What do sequential abilities mean?**
> This skill deals with understanding the events of the narrative according to its sequential order of sections, sentences and words that create the entire narrative.
> This skill can be exercised by analyzing the sequences of segments, key sentences and keywords and by naming its segments according to their sequence.

The Tortoise and the Hare
by Aesop

The tortoise did not pay attention and plodded heavily forward, which made the hare even more scornful and laugh even harder. The tortoise was laboriously plodding along while the hare yelled at him:
"When I hit the road, I'll make the dust fly! Hurry up, otherwise it will take the whole night to end this thing."
"That's alright with me, don't move a muscle, hare," the tortoise breathed heavily, and made his way slowly but confidently. "You can say what you please, but I'm going to leave you in the dust. We shall see who the winner will be!"
"You, beat me?! Ha, that's hilarious! What nonsense! Who ever heard of a tortoise that can outrun a hare? I can take you over however I want and in any event I will!"
The tortoise heard that, kept his mouth shut, and laboriously continued ploddingly away.

Light-footed is the hare, quick-witted is the tortoise.

One day the nimble hare said to the plodding tortoise, "Let's have a race. The one that finishes first will win the victory cup."

Surely enough, he was convinced that no one could beat him, because he was the swiftest of runners, everybody knew that.

"Okay," said the tortoise. "I accept your challenge; we shall see who has the last laugh. There, at the end of the road, is the finish line!"

The hare, brimming with self-confidence, did not even bother to step up to the starting point. Instead he leaned back on the roadside and taunted the tortoise: "Move it kiddo, move it!"

When the hare opened his eyes, what did he see? The tortoise had almost reached the finish line; only a little step separated him from it.

Leaping up high, as fast as the wind, the hare started to sprint, but all for nothing, he was too late. The tortoise took one little step further; he reached the finish line first, and won the victory cup.

"You see," concluded the tortoise, "Next time, dear friend, don't waste words; actions speak louder than words."

"The poor thing has not even made it half way. Meanwhile I will take a little nap, because I can always beat him," muttered the hare and lay down to sleep.

While the hare was napping, his snoring sounded like sneering, jeering at the efforts of the tortoise.

 ## B. Sequence of Pictures

1. The following pictures are not in the correct order. Number each one according to the sequence of the narrative.

2. Insert the following key sentences below each picture.

What is a key sentence?
A key sentence is the most important sentence in each paragraph. Without a key sentence a paragraph might become meaningless.

The hare leaned back on the roadside and taunted the tortoise.
The hare said to the tortoise: "race with me."
He was convinced that no one could beat him.
"I accept your challenge."
The tortoise plodded slowly.
The tortoise made his way slowly but confidently.
You can talk as you please, but I'm going to leave you in the dust.
The race began.
Nonsense.
The tortoise won the victory cup.
Meanwhile I would take a little nap, because I can always beat him.

3. Copy the above sentences according to their right sequence of appearance in the story.

1. _____
2. _____
3. _____
4. _____
5. _____
6. _____
7. _____
8. _____
9. _____
10. _____
11. _____

4. Embed the following keywords according to their sequence in the picture:

What is a keyword?
Keywords are the main words in a sentence. Without keywords the sentence might become meaningless.
To locate these words one must raise the following two questions:
A. To whom does the sentence refer?
B. What does the key sentence refer to?

Lie down	Laboriously and ploddingly	Race with me
Taunted	Talk as you please	Plodded slowly
I will leave you in the dust	Tortoise	Take a little nap
Hare	Was too late	Always beat him
Actions speak	Confidently	Don't waste words
But all for nothing	Victory cup	Opened his eyes
	Almost reaching	

5. Create three questions for each of the following sentences:

A. When the hare opened his eyes he realized that the tortoise had almost reached the finish line.

B. The hare leaned back at the roadside.

C. "Okay" said the tortoise. "I accept your challenge. There, at the end of the road, is the finish line!"

1. What: _____

2. Who: _____

3. Where: _____

 # Verbal Understanding

> **What does the skill of locating details entail?**
> This skill deals with the minute details of the narrative and can be practiced using the following questions:
> 1. Who said this to whom?
> 2. What could replace what they said? (what is trying to be said? i.e What's another way of saying the same thing?)
> 3. True or false?
> 4. Classification tables

B. Locating Details

1. The following sentences have been mixed up. Match each sentence with its correct ending:

And taunted the tortoise _____

He was convinced _____

The first one to get _____

But all for nothing. _____

Actions speak _____

You can say what you want _____

Louder than words _____

Leave you in the dust _____

Slowly but confidently _____

Fast as the wind _____

Would win the victory cup _____

I can always beat him _____

The tortoise was plodding laboriously _____

I will take a little nap _____

Lay back by the side of the road _____

 Students will retell the story in their own words and present the story in their own language. Students will stage a skit for the class – playing characters from the story.

Language Enrichment

A. Check the right meaning of the following phrases:

Opened his eyes
- 1. Closed his eyes
- 2. Woke up ← (selected)
- 3. Cried
- 4. Looked upward

Jeering
- 1. Sneering
- 2. All for nothing
- 3. Careless
- 4. Slowly

As you please
- 1. Wariness
- 2. Breathless
- 3. As you wish
- 4. Benevolence

Quick-witted
- 1. Stupid
- 2. Hard-worker
- 3. Nimble
- 4. Wise

Didn't make an effort
- 1. Tried hard
- 2. Didn't think it was important

B. Some words in the following paragraph were deleted. Insert the right word in the story.

The hare lay down to sleep. When the hare opened his eyes, what did he see? The tortoise was almost _____ finish line. Leaping up high, as fast as the wind, the hare _____ but it was in vain, he was too late. The tortoise _____ a little step further. He reached the finish line first, and _____ the victory cup.

Causal Clauses

> Causal Clauses—what do they mean?
> Causal clauses can be classified into three types: fact, causal words, causality.
> Causal words can include conjunctions such as: *as, since, thus, for, hence.*

The following sentences are factual and causal clauses. Pair each causal cause with its factual complement.

* The tortoise won the race _____.
* The hare challenged the tortoise to race with him _____.
* _____ as he was sure no one could beat him.
* _____ since he plodded slowly but confidently.
* The hare decided to take a little nap, _____.
* _____, for he was convinced he could always beat the tortoise.
* The hare lost the race _____.
* _____ , since he was napping.
* The hare decided to take a little nap _____.
* _____ since he was sure that he can always go past the tortoise.

C. Change the following sentences from singular to plural:

Example: the hare is light-footed → the hares are light-footed

1. The one who finishes first.
2. I accept your challenge.
3. He leaned back at the roadside.
4. I will take a little nap.
5. Leaping up high, as fast as the wind, the hare ran.

D. Change the following sentences from past to present tense:

Example: The nimble hare said to the plodding tortoise/The nimble hare says to the plodding tortoise.

1. He was convinced that no one could beat him.
2. Did not even make it half way.
3. Muttered the hare and lay down to sleep.
4. When the hare opened his eyes he saw that the tortoise had almost reached the finish line.
5. The hare yelled at him.

_____

_____

_____

_____

_____

_____

_____

_____

_____

_____

E. Complete the Crossword Puzzle

Horizontally:

1. sleep
2. jog
3. the ending point of a competition
4. running slowly
5. turtle
6. rabbit
7. running with full speed
8. competition

Vertically:

9. the hare, when seeing the tortoise on the finish line started to ….
10. laughter
11. very quick
12. the price the tortoise took
13. ran faster than
14. opposite of fault

Fill in the crossword puzzle.

"Why Are the Leaves of the Tree Blue?" by Valentina Oseeva

The teacher will read the story in class.

1. Ofra had two green pencils.
   Ilana did not have any pencils.
   Ilana asked Ofra,
   "Will you lend me a green pencil?"
   Ofra replied,
   "I must ask my mom."

2. The next day Ilana asked Ofra,
   "Did you ask your mom?"
   Ofra answered,
   "My mom gave me permission,
   but I did not ask my brother."
   Ilana told her,
   "You can ask your brother too."

3. The next day Ilana asked Ofra,
   "Well, did your brother give you permission?"
   Ofra retorted,
   "Yes, my brother gave me permission,
   but I'm afraid that you might break the pencil."
   Ilana promised Ofra,
   "I will draw carefully."

   Ofra allowed her to borrow the green pencil.
   She said,
   "Do not sharpen the pencil,
   or press it too hard.
   Do not put it in your mouth.
   Do not draw with it too much."

4. Ilana said to her,
   "I just need to use the green
   for painting the tree's leaves
   and some grass."
   Ofra answered,
   "That's too much."
   Ilana turned and went away
   without taking the pencil.

5. Ofra was agitated.
   She ran after Ilana.
   She called Ilana,
   "What happened?
   Take the pencil with you!"
   Ilana muttered shortly,
   "I do not need your pencil!"

6. The teacher asked Ilana during the lesson,
   "Why did you color the tree's leaves in blue?"
   Ilana answered,
   "Because I do not have a green pencil."
   The teacher enquired further,
   "So why didn't you borrow one from your friend, Ofra?"
   Ilana was quiet and did not answer.
   Ofra blushed and said quietly,

7. "I wanted to give it to Ilana,
   but she did not want to take it."

8. The teacher looked at the two girls.
   "A person is obliged to give in a way that encourages the other to take."

Verbal Understanding

Mapping Out of Concepts

What does the skill of mapping out of concepts means?
Practicing the skill of mapping out of concepts endows the written story with a format of a graphical map of keywords that are embedded in a map. Practicing this skill is done by using flow charts, venn diagrams and diffuse mapping.

"Diffuse Mapping"—Diffuse Mapping + classifications

A. Go back to the story "Why Are the Leaves of the Tree Blue?" on page 46 and read it carefully.

B. The Diffuse Mapping illustration below is connected with the issue of *friendship*. Add words that connote this issue and connect you with it. Write them down on the yellow "sun rays" below.

C. Classify the wording of your Diffuse Mapping according to the following table:

True Friendship	Disappointing Friendship	Feelings

 # Sequence

 ## Segments of Meaning

> **What do sequential abilities mean?**
> This skill deals with understanding the events of the narrative according to the sequential order of sections, sentences and words that create the entire narrative.
> This skill can be exercised by analyzing the sequences of segments, key sentences and keywords by naming its segments according to sequence.

A. The following paragraphs are not in the correct order. Rearrange them in the correct order by giving each paragraph a number.

B. Circle each keyword that is inside a key sentence.

C. Add conjunctions.

Ilana asks Ofra to lend her a pencil
and Ofra rejects her for the second time.

Ofra tried to appease Ilana
but Ilana did not take the pencil.

The teacher asked Ilana during the lesson,
"Why did you color the tree's leaves in blue?"
Ilana answered, "Because I do not have a green pencil."
Ofra said. "I wanted to give it to Ilana, but she did not want to take it."

> Ilana asks to borrow a pencil from Ofra
> and Ofra rejects her for the third time now.
> Ofra agrees to lend her the pencil, gives her warnings.

> Ilana turns away without taking the pencil.

> Ofra has two green pencils.
> Ilana does not have a green pencil.
> Ilana asks Ofra to lend her a pencil
> and Ofra rejects her for the first time.

> The teacher says, "A person should give in a way that makes the other person want to take."

D. Sum up the story by using keywords and conjunctions.

 ## Raising and Classifying Questions

 **What does the skill of raising questions mean?**
This skill deals with raising questions on three levels of thinking: verbal, interpretive and implemental. To practice this skill, use WH-words such as who, what, how much, where, where to, why and whether as well as what did they feel? What is your opinion? What would you do if …? etc.

Write twelve questions about the story.

1. _____
2. _____
3. _____
4. _____
5. _____
6. _____
7. _____
8. _____
9. _____
10. _____
11. _____
12. _____

* The teacher will hold a discussion in class about Ofra's conduct and students will be asked to give their opinion.
* Students will use tape recorders to record similar stories of children and adults.
* Students will create a comic skit using visual and verbal tools and write various thoughts and feelings in balloons on cards.

1. Classify your questions by using the following table:

An answer exists in the fable	An answer does not exist in the fable

2. Classify your prepared questions according to the general titles:

Verbal-understanding questions	Interpretive-understanding questions	Implemental questions

Circle verbal understanding WH-words in **green**.
Circle interpretive-understanding WH-words in **red**.
Circle implemental WH-words in **blue**.

3. Classify your questions according to the following table:

Emotional questions	Critical and judgmental questions	Emphatic questions

 **Mapping Out of Concepts**

 **What does the skill of mapping out of concepts mean?**
Practicing the skill of mapping out of concepts formats the written story graphical map by using keywords that are embedded in this map. This skill is practiced by using flow charts, Venn Diagrams and Diffuse Mapping.

 Flow Chart

1. Re-read the story on page 50.
2. The flow chart below is partially filled with key sentences.
3. Complete the flow chart with some additional key sentences. You can use the kit of key sentences on the next page.

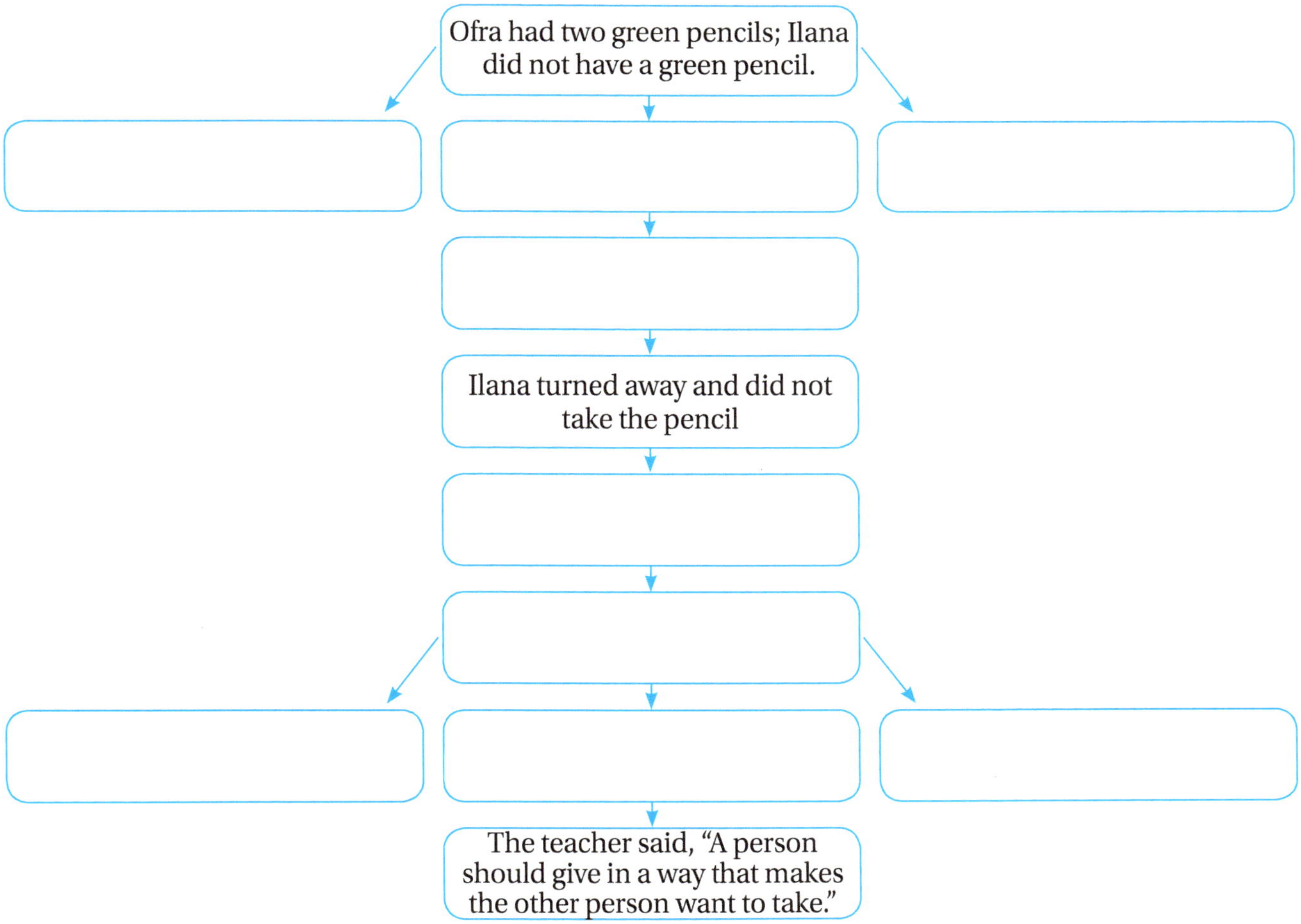

- Ofra had two green pencils; Ilana did not have a green pencil.
- Ilana turned away and did not take the pencil
- The teacher said, "A person should give in a way that makes the other person want to take."

- Ilana asks Ofra to lend her a pencil and Ofra rejects her for the first time.
- Ofra tried to appease Ilana but Ilana did not take the pencil.
- Ofra said, "I wanted to give it to Ilana, but she did not want to take it."
- Ilana asks Ofra to lend her a pencil and Ofra rejects her for the second time.
- The teacher said, "A person should give in a way that makes the other person want to take."
- Ilana replied, "Because I don't have a green pencil."
- Ofra agrees to lend her the pencil, but gives her warnings.
- Ilana turns away without taking the pencil.
- The teacher asked, "Why are the leaves of the tree blue?"
- Ofra had two green pencils; Ilana did not have a green pencil.
- Ilana asks to borrow a pencil from Ofra and Ofra rejects her for the third time now.

Linguistic Enrichment

1. Locate nouns, verbs, and adjectives in the story.
2. Classify the words you find in the table below:

Nouns	Verbs	Adjectives

3. Classify the nouns you find as singulars and plurals:

Singular	Plural

4. **Classify the verbs in the story as full and auxiliary verbs (helping verbs, for example—can, should, be, must, would).**

Full verbs	Auxiliary verbs

5. **Classify the verbs in the story as past, present and future tenses.**

Past	Present	Future

Why Does the Ox Walk Slowly?

Many, many years ago man searched for an animal that could carry heavy weights and finally he found the ox.
The hard-working, good-natured ox began to carry heavy loads on its back while walking at a fast pace.

The ox had been carrying heavy loads for one, two and three years until he could tolerate no more of this work, so he asked the man, "Please tell me, man. When will you put an end to my hard work?" The man answered, "This hard work of yours will never stop. You will have to lug this heavy weight around for the rest of your life."

Hearing this, the ox halted and pondered, "If I'm going to carry such a heavy weight for the rest of my life without getting any rest, why should I hurry? It would be better to do the work very slowly. I'm never going to finish it anyway."

And from that day onward the ox has walked slowly.

Verbal Understanding

A. In the following passage some of the words are missing. Fill the missing words in the blanks.

What does a deficient passage mean? (Cloze paragraphs)
The skill of filling in a deficient passage enables a learner to replace missing words by relying on contextual clues. A student can base his or her filling in on previous knowledge and textual context or by citing a word from the text.

Why Does the Ox Walk Slowly?

Many, many years ago a man searched for an animal that could _____ heavy weights and finally he found _____ .
The hard-working, good-natured ox began to carry immensely _____ loads on its back while walking at a fast pace.

The ox had been carrying heavy loads for one, two and three years until eventually he _____ this work anymore, so he asked the man, "Please tell me, man. _____ put an end to my hard work?" The man answered, "_____ will never stop. You will have to lug _____ weight around for the rest of your life."

Hearing this, the ox halted and pondered, "If I'm going to carry such a heavy weight for the rest of my life without getting _____ why should I hurry? It would be better to do the work _____ slowly. I'm never going to _____ it anyway."

And from that day onward the ox has walked slowly.

List of missing words: when, to carry, the ox, very, heavy, rest, could tolerate no more, heavy, this hard work of yours, finish.

B. Classify the words you have filled in the deficient passage as nouns, verbs and adjectives.

Nouns	Verbs	Adjectives

C. Copy the sentence with the main idea, namely, the principle sentence of the story that holds most of the fable's keywords.

_____
_____
_____
_____
_____
_____
_____
_____

# Interpretive Understanding

 Questions that have something to do with the main idea of the story:

A. Why would the ox's work never be stopped?

B. Why did the ox decide to walk slowly?

C. Why should he not hurry?

D. What conclusion can you make about the ox's wisdom?

E. How is the ox characterized in the story?

 **Implementation**

A. What would you suggest that the ox do?

_____

_____

B. In your opinion, was the ox's conclusion right?

_____

_____

> **What does the skill of distinguishing between fact and opinion mean?**
> This skill distinguishes between personal opinions and attitudes toward an event, occasion and data. To exercise this skill, use phrases such as: I think that…, In my opinion…. or Perhaps it should…
> Fact means telling the narrative without supplementing it with personal interpretations and descriptions. To practice this skill, use phrases such as "The story tells that…" or "The story implicates that…"

C. Classify the following sentences as facts and opinions:

1. "The ox was strong."

2. "The ox carries heavy loads."

3. "The ox is a hard-worker."

4. "He carried and hauled until he could tolerate no more of this work."

5. "Why should I hurry then?"

6. "It would be better to do the work very slowly."

7. "I'm never going to finish it."

8. "And from that day onward the ox walks slowly."

Facts	Opinions verbs

 Students will conduct internet and encyclopedia research to learn about the characteristics of an ox and will share the information about its unique attributes with the class.

A Nice Tale that Happened in our Town
by Danny Kerman

In our town there used to live a poor husband and his wife. They saved every penny, until they had collected enough money and decided to open a shop for selling fish. They searched and found a place near the river and built a nice stand there. They bought a scale, ordered some wooden barrels and stocked them up with fresh fish. Early in the morning the husband went and hung a large, shiny sign above the opening of the shop:

"Fish for Sale – Here."

When his wife woke up, she looked at her husband's handiwork and burst out laughing.

"What are you laughing at?" asked the husband.

"Why in the world did you write the word h*ere*?" answered the wife laughing.

"Could it cross anyone's mind that you are advertising fish that are being sold in another city? It's clear that they are being sold right here."

"Well; you are a wise wife," answered the husband. He took a bucket full of paint and painted over the word *here*."

Once again the wife gazed at the sign and declared, "And the words *for sale*—what are they for? Could anybody believe that we deliver fish for free?"

"Well," said the husband. "Indeed, you are a brilliant woman!" He climbed up and painted over the words *for sale*. Shortly afterward, while still descending from the ladder, his wife scrutinized the sign again and remarked,

"What do we need the word *fish* for? Will anyone conceive that we opened a shop near the river to sell precious stones and diamonds?"

"Your wisdom is infallible," replied the husband, and erased the word *fish* from the sign. Now the couple examined the nice sign with a self-satisfied smirk.

They sat down and waited for customers to come in.

And they are still waiting until this very day.

Verbal Understanding

1. Developing of sequential abilities

What do sequential abilities mean?

This skill deals with understanding the events of the narrative according to its sequential order of sections, sentences and words that create the entire narrative.

This skill can be exercised by analyzing the sequences of segments, key sentences and keywords and by naming its segments according to their sequence.

A. Read the following passages. Reorganize and number each paragraph according to its correct order in the content of the story.

> When his wife woke up, she looked at her husband's handiwork and burst out laughing.
> "What are you laughing at?" asked the husband.
> "Why in the world did you write the word *here*?" answered the wife laughing.
> "Could it cross anyone's mind that you are advertising fish that are being sold in another city? It's clear-cut that they are being sold right here."
> "Well, you are a wise wife," answered the husband. He took a bucket full of paint and painted over the word *here*."

FISH FOR SALE HERE

In our town there used to live a poor husband and his wife. They saved every penny, until they had collected enough money and decided to open a shop for selling fish. They searched and found a place near the river and built a nice stand there. They bought a scale, ordered some wooden barrels and stocked them up with fresh fish. Early in the morning the husband went and hung a big, bold sign above the opening of the shop:

Once again the wife gazed at the sign and declared: "And the words *for sale*—what are they for? Could anybody believe that we deliver fish for free?"
"Well," said the husband. "Indeed, you are a brilliant woman!" He climbed up and painted over the words *for sale*.

Now the couple examined the nice sign with a self-satisfied smirk.
They sat down and waited for customers to come in.
And they are still waiting until this very day.

Shortly afterward, while still descending from the ladder, his wife scrutinized the sign again and remarked, "What do we need the word *fish* for? Will anyone conceive that we opened a shop near the river to sell precious stones and diamonds?"
"Your wisdom is infallible," replied the husband, and erased the word *fish* from the sign.

B. Locate one or more key sentences in each paragraph and write them down below according to their sequence.

C. Answer the following questions:

1. Who used to live in our town?

2. What did the couple decide to open?

3. What was written on the sign the husband hung above the opening of the shop?

4. What did the wife tell her husband about the word *here*?

5. What did the wife tell her husband about the words *'for sale'*?

6. What did the wife tell her husband about the word *'fish'*?

7. For whom is the couple waiting?

8. Did any customers eventually come into their shop?

 ## 2. Skill of Locating Details

A. Write true or false next to the following sentences:

2. In our town there used to live a rich husband and his wife. _____

3. He took a bucket full of paint and painted over the word *'here'*. _____

4. He climbed up and painted over the words *'for sale'*. _____

5. And opened a shop that sold precious stones and diamonds. _____

6. Many customers came to the shop. _____

B. A word and its antonym—write the antonyms (words with the opposite meaning) **next to the following list:**

Rich people _____

Fresh fish _____

Sellers _____

Wise woman _____

For free _____

We opened _____

Customers _____

Climbed up _____

 ### 3. Classifications

A. Sort out the wife and husband's sentences.

What the wife said	What the husband said

 ### 4. Flow Chart

 **What does flow chart mean?**
A flow chart can be used for organizing information and for tracking genres with plots and sequence of events or for scientific texts with cause and effect. It can be used by embedding keywords in the chart.

1. The following flow chart graphically portrays the developments of Danny Kerman's tale.
2. The flow chart below is partially filled with key sentences; read them.
3. Fill in the flow chart with some additional key sentences. Use the kit of key sentences on page 72.

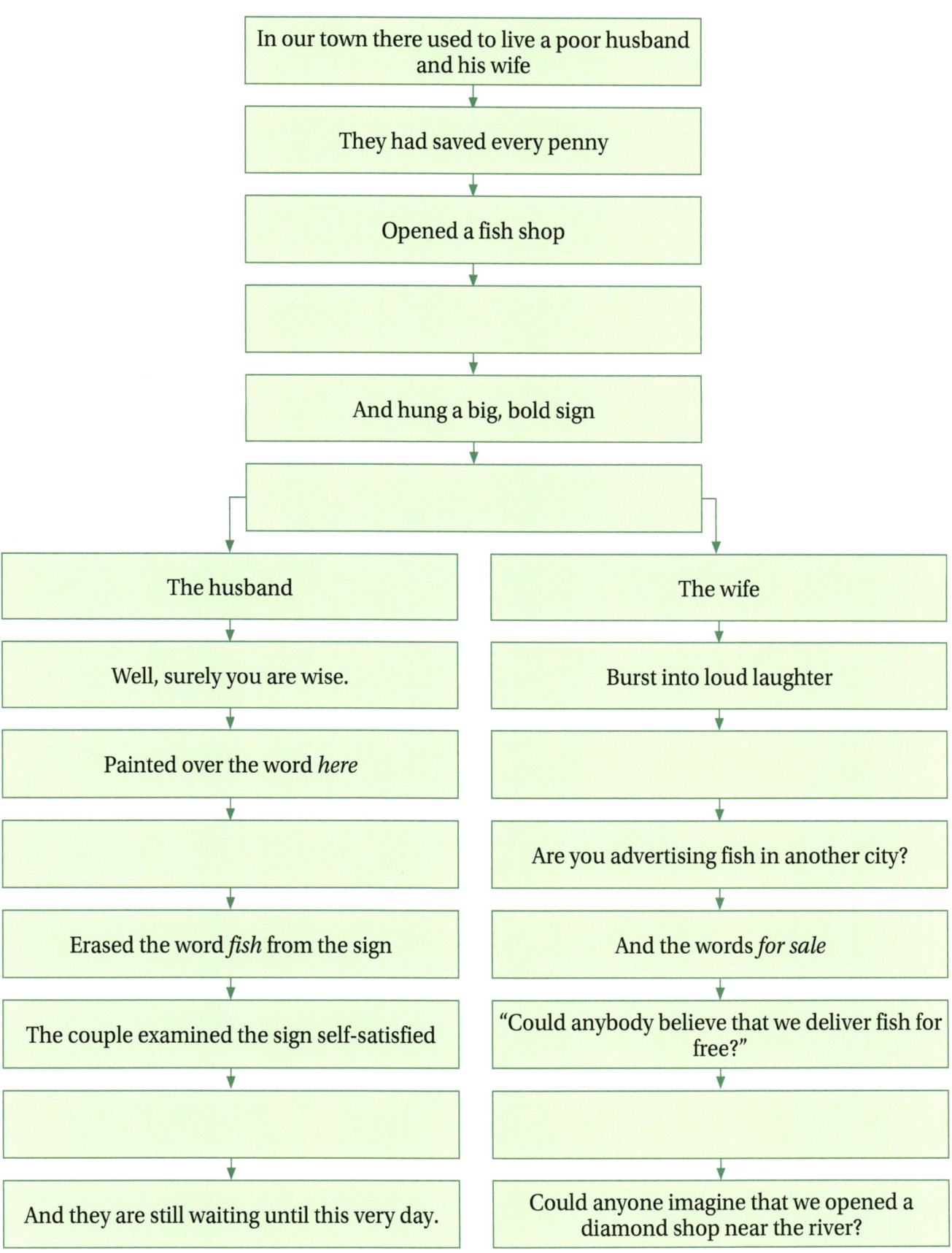

Kit of keywords:

1. Ordered barrels and stocked them with fish
2. Fish for Sale–Here
3. Why did you write –*here?*
4. Well, you are wise
5. Why do we need *fish*?
6. Waiting for customers

 ## The Skill of Summarization

 **What does the skill of summarization mean?**
This skill deals with writing a main synopsis out of the literary text. The skill can be practiced using keywords, key sentences and conjunctions.

Sum up the flow chart by using keywords and key sentences and by linking them with conjunctions.

Interpretative Understanding

A. Locating a main idea in the text that is not stated explicitly.

What does an implicit main idea mean?
This skill deals with identifying a main idea that is not stated explicitly in the text. It can be exercised by raising questions about a main idea that holds a wealth of keywords that were already identified in the text. This can be done by using WH-words like why, how, whether and which.

1. "Indeed, you are a brilliant woman," said the husband. Do you agree with his assertion and believe that she was brilliant?

   _____
   _____
   _____
   _____
   _____

2. And they are still waiting until this very day…

   Why do you think they are still waiting?

   Give three reasons to support your answer:

   1. _____
   2. _____
   3. _____

 **B. Analyzing Characters.**

Refer to the classification table on page 71. Reread the wife's lines and compare them with her husband's actions. What can you learn from this about the husband's personality in comparison with that of the wife's? Use the stock of human traits below:

Wife's traits	Husband's traits

List of human traits: wise, submissive, overbearing, admiring, sarcastic, hardworking, lazy.

# Implementation

## 1. Problem Solving

> **What does problem solving mean?**
> This skill deals with solving applied problems that may be implicated from the text. The skill could be practiced by asking emphatic questions like, 'What would you do instead?' 'Would you do the same?' or 'Which tip would you give the character?'
> Another method is by raising judicial and critical questions like: 'Was he right in your opinion?' or 'Would you behave in the same manner as them?'
> In addition there are emotive questions like, 'How did you feel?' 'What made you sad?' or 'What made you happy?'

What would you write on the sign if you were to open a fish shop?

Support your sign with arguments.

Implementation

A. What preparations would you make if you were to open a fish shop?

_____
_____
_____

B. Prepare a sign for your shop.

_____
_____
_____

C. Why do you need a sign for your shop?

_____
_____
_____

D. Which tip would you give the husband about the fish shop?

_____
_____
_____

E. Which tip would you give the wife?

_____
_____
_____

* Students will orally report about the sequence of events in the story.
* Students will make a list of directions for a "shop launching" event.
* Students will make up a "menu" for a "fish restaurant".

The Sweetest Music in the World
A Persian folktale

One day the king of Persia asked his ministers, "What is the sweetest music in the world?" The ministers started to argue about the answer. One said, "The sound of a flute is the sweetest." Another opposed him with, "The sound of a violin is the sweetest." And a third preferred the sound of a harp. Only minister Mirza, the wisest minister of all, sat quietly. Not long after that, Mirza invited the king and his ministers to a party, and indeed was it a nice party. Famous musicians played pleasant melodies for the guests with a flute, a violin and a harp and they entertained the guests greatly. However, food was not served at the table. The guests hunger grew bigger and bigger, and then, the sound of a tablespoon hitting a plate was heard from the far end of the hall. The guests were able to breath with relief now; at last it was almost dinnertime!

Minister Mirza laughed and asked his guests, "What is the sweetest music in the world?"

The king answered, "There is no music as sweet as the sound of a tablespoon hitting a plate to the ear of a hungry man."

 ## Verbal Understanding

 ### 1. Developing of sequential abilities

What does sequence mean?
A sequence of sections is the paragraphs that come one after the other and allow for students to make a deduction [assumption] about the development of narrative.

A. Read the story, "The Sweetest Music in the World."

B. Divide the story into five parts.

C. Name each part.

1. _____

2. _____

3. _____

4. _____

5. _____

D. Read the names of the sequences of the segments and answer:

Can you learn about the contents of the story from the names you've given to the segments? Explain.

_____

_____

_____

_____

 ## 2. Key Sentences in Sequence

 **What does a key sentence mean?**
A key sentence is the most significant sentence in a paragraph. Without it the paragraph becomes meaningless.

A. Some of the story's key sentences are listed below. Arrange them in the right sequence according to the content of the story.

B. Match key sentences to the segment names you have chosen.

1. "At last it was almost dinnertime!"

2. "Mirza invited the king and his ministers to a nice party."

3. "What is the sweetest music in the world?"

4. "Only Minister Mirza, the wisest minister, sat quietly."

5. "The sound of a tablespoon hitting a plate was heard."

6. "There is no music as sweet as the sound of a tablespoon hitting a plate to the ear of a hungry man."

7. "The ministers started to argue about the issue."

8. "Food was not served at the table."

1. _____
2. _____
3. _____
4. _____
5. _____
6. _____
7. _____
8. _____

C. Read the key sentences out loud.

D. Locate in each key sentence its keywords. List and add them to the key sentences.

What is a keyword?

Keywords are the main words in a sentence and without them it might be meaningless.

To locate these words, one must raise the following two questions:
a. To whom does the sentence refer?
b. What does the sentence refer to?

A sequence of key sentences:

_____

_____

_____

_____

A sequence of keywords:

_____

_____

_____

_____

Raising and Classifying Questions

A. Raise questions at all three levels of thinking about the story. Raise two questions for each WH-word.

_____

_____

_____

_____

_____

_____

_____

_____

Verbal thinking	Interpretive thinking	Implementation
Who?	Whether?	What do you think…?
What?	Why?	What would you do instead…?
How many?	Which?	How does he feel…?
Where?	How?	Whether he was right…?
Where to?	How?	How did you feel…?

B. Classify the questions you've raised in the following table according to their WH-words:

Who?	What?	How many?	Where?	How?	Why?	Whether?

C. Classify the questions according to the three levels of thinking:

Verbal thinking	Interpretive thinking	Implementation

D. Classify the questions in the following table:

An answer exists in the text	An answer does not exist in the text

The Skill of Locating Details

A. Who said this to whom?

"What is the sweetest music in the world?"
_____

"At last it was almost dinnertime!"
_____

"The sound of a flute is the sweetest."
_____

"There is no music as sweet as the sound of a tablespoon hitting a plate to the ear of a hungry man."
_____

B. What was originally written in the text?

Important musicians played to the guests _____
_____

The bang of a tablespoon on a plate _____
_____

They were eased _____
_____

C. Write true or false.

1. Food was served to the guests. _____
_____

2. There is no music as sweet as the sound of a tablespoon hitting a plate to the ear of a hungry man. _____

3. The ministers started to argue about the issue. _____

4. Only Minister Mirza spoke. _____

D. Classify the keywords (page 78) according to the table below.

List the sentences that refer to each character:

King of Persia	Ministers	Minister Mirza

 ## The Skill of Locating a Main Idea

> **What does the skill of locating the main idea mean?**
> The meaning of locating the main idea in a text is finding sentences that hold the most important idea. To exercise this skill we must locate most of the keywords in the sentences.

A. Locate the sentence that holds most of the keywords and copy it.

_____
_____

B. What is the name of a sentence that holds most of keywords?

_____
_____

 # Linguistic Enrichment

A. Locate nouns, verbs and adjectives in the key sentences. Classify them in the table below:

Nouns	Verbs	Adjectives

B. Make four sentences using causal clauses and connect them to the content of the story.

For example: Minister Mirza kept quiet **because** he was wise.

Note: Causal clauses are divided into three parts: fact, causal word, causality.

Causal Clauses—what do they mean?

Causal clauses can be classified into three types: fact, causal words, causality.

Causal words may include conjunctions such as: *as, since, thus, for, hence.*

1. _____
2. _____
3. _____
4. _____

 **Cloze**

Fill in the blanks of the following deficient passage with verbs:

One day the King of Persia _____ his ministers, "What is the sweetest music in the world?" The ministers _____ about the issue. One _____, and a third _____ preferred the sound of a harp. Only Minister Mirza, the wisest minister of all, _____. Not long after, Mirza _____ the king and ministers to a party, and indeed _____ a nice party. Famous musicians _____ for the guests nice melodies with flute, violin and harp.

 **Explicit Content Clues**

Add synonyms:

 Explicit content clues are clues within the text that help us understand the story by examining synonyms, antonyms and explanations.

1. Minister Mirza was wise and _____ .
2. The party was nice and _____ .
3. The musicians were celebrated and _____ .
4. Each knock and _____ of a tablespoon hitting a plate.
5. The ministers started to argue and _____ about the issue.

List of missing words: luxurious, bang, debate, clever, famous.

 # Interpretative Understanding

 Locating a main idea in the text that is not stated explicitly.

 **What does an explicit main idea mean?**
This skill enables us to identify a main idea that is not stated explicitly in the text. It can be practiced by posing questions about the main idea using keywords. This can be done by using WH questions like why, how, whether and which.

A. The sentence below expresses the main idea of the story:

> "There is no music as sweet as the sound of a tablespoon hitting a plate to the ear of a hungry man."

B. Raise questions about this main idea that have answers that cannot be found in the story.

C. Use the following WH-words: why, how, which, whether, what.

> Note: You can also raise questions that you don't know the answers to.

1. What? _____ What is the sweetest music in the world? _____
2. Why? _____
3. How? _____
4. Which? _____
5. Whether? _____
6. Where? _____

D. Answer the questions you have raised:

5. _____

6. _____

7. _____

8. _____

9. _____

10. _____

 **Predicting Events**

> **What does predicting events mean?**
> This ability deals with predicting both the end of a story and some of its parts. It can be exercised through using clues such as: the name of the story, the story without its end, only its end or by completing some of its parts.
> An accurate prediction of events is possible only if a student already understands the explicit parts of the story.

Try to think of a different end to the story "The Sweetest Music in the World."

_____
_____
_____

 **Identifying the Author's Viewpoint**

A. Is the author's conclusion about the sweetest music correct?

_____
_____
_____
_____
_____

 # Implementation

A. What do you believe is the sweetest music in the world? Why?

B. What happens to you when you are hungry?

C. What would you do if you were hungry but no food was available?

---

* The students will stage the story and portray its various dramatic roles.
* The students will retell the story as if it were a journalistic newsreel.

Keep an Eye on the Door
A Jewish-Iraqi folktale

The parents of the Baghdadi fool, Husham, went to the market and told him, "Keep an eye on the door until we get back." "All right," said Husham.

Not long after they left Husham turned to the door, took it off its hinges and moved it into the room, where he sat and watched it. A burglar that was passing by realized the house had been broken into. He entered it and pilfered whatever he could put his hands on and left. The parents returned home and alas! The house had been burglarized and all of their possessions were gone. They asked Husham, "What have you done? Why didn't you keep your eye on the door?" Husham answered, "Here it is; I sat and watched it the whole time."

Verbal Understanding

Developing Abilities of Sequence

A. Carefully read the story *Keep an Eye on the Door*.

B. The following keyword list is mixed up. Rearrange them in the right order according to the content of the story by changing the sequence of numbers.

What is a keyword?
Keywords are the main words in a sentence and without them it might be meaningless.
To locate these words one must raise the following two questions:
a. To whom does the sentence refer?
b. What does the sentence refer to?

1. Keep an eye on
2. I watched it
3. His parents had left
4. All the time
5. Door
6. Room
7. Moved into
8. Why didn't you keep your eye on the door
9. The parents returned
10. A burglar was passing
11. Entered
12. A burglarized house
13. Took it off its hinges

C. Sum up the content of the story by using keywords and add conjunctions.

Summarization of content of the story:

# The Skill of Locating Details

A. Who said that to whom?

"Keep an eye on the door until we are back."
_____

"All right" _____

"Why didn't you keep your eye on the door?"
_____

"I sat and watched it the whole time."
_____

B. What was said instead?

Remove it from its place
_____
_____

Everything that was in the house
_____
_____

Dear me!
_____
_____

 ## Classifications

Indicate which characters in the story the keyword refers to:

Husham's parents	The burglar	Husham

 ## Locating a Main Idea

What does a main idea mean?
The main idea of the story is a key sentence that contains keywords.

The following keywords compose the main idea of the story, but they are mixed up. Piece these words into a sequence of a main idea sentence.

> Keep an eye, burglar, took off, everything in the house, why didn't you keep your eye? door, the whole time, I watched it.

Verbal Enrichment

A. Locate the verbs from the story and classify them according to the following table:

Verb	Tense	Person
Example: Went	*Example:* Past	*Example:* They

B. A Linguistic Construct: verb + preposition

Add a preposition to the verbs you listed in the table above.

Example: went + to…. Looked + at

Prepositions can be:, at, under, above, between, inside of, outside of, next out

_____

_____

_____

_____

C. Make five sentences that are based on the verb + preposition linguistic construct.

Example: Husham **turned to** the door.

1. _____
2. _____

3. _____

4. _____

5. _____

Explicit Content Clues—Explanation Clues

Circle the explanation words you locate in the following sentences:

> **What does explanation mean?**
> An explanation interprets difficult words and is marked up by an em-dash.

1. Not long after they left Husham turned to the door, <u>took it off its hinges</u>—took the door forcefully from its place.

2. A burglar that was passing by realized the <u>house was broken into</u>—the door was wide open.

3. Entered it, stole whatever he <u>could put his hands on</u>—everything he could take.

4. Why didn't you keep <u>your eye</u> on the door?"—did not look at the door.

D. Write in which things explanation marks can help in understanding the sentence.

_____

_____

_____

Interpret the following words:
Broken into _____ , tore _____ , put his hands on _____

 # Interpretative Understanding

 ### The Skill of Predicting Events

A. Try to compose an alternative end to the story.

 **An Implicit Main Idea**

 **What does an implicit main idea mean?**
This skill deals with identifying a main idea that is not stated implicitly in the text. It can be exercised by raising questions about a main idea that holds a wealth of keywords that were already identified in the text. This can be done by using WH-words like why, how, whether and which.

A. The four following sentences are from the story.

B. Read the sentences and raise questions that you don't know the answers to. Use WH-words.

1. Not long after they left, Husham turned to the door, took it off its hinges and moved it into the room.

2. A burglar that was passing by realized the house had been broken into, entered it, and pilfered whatever he could put his hands on.

3. "What have you done? Why didn't you keep your eye on the door?"

4. "Here it is; I sat and watched it the whole time."

What? _____

Why? _____

How? _____

Which? _____

Whether? _____

_____

C. Answer the questions you composed.

_____

_____

_____

_____

D. What can you learn about Husham's character from the answers he gave his parents?

_____

_____

_____

_____

Implementation

A. What would you have done if your parents had asked you to "keep an eye on the door until we get back"?

_____

_____

_____

B. What would you recommend Husham to do?

_____

_____

_____

C. What do you know about Husham tales? What type of tales are they?

* Students will tell more Husham jokes.
* The teacher will bring joke books to class and the students will point out different types of humor.

Alternative Assessment:
Indicator of Reading and Comprehension on Three Levels of Thinking

Student name: _____ Class: _____ School: _____ Level of implementation: _____

Literal understanding	Starting out	Progress achieving the goal	Achieving the goal
Sequence	Did not understand the meaning of the sequence and did not accomplish assignments that associate with sequence of segments, key sentences and keywords.	Partly understood sequential assignments and partly achieved them.	Understood the meaning of sequential narrative and accomplished all assignments associated with sequence of segments, key sentences and keywords.
Detail locating	Did not locate details of the following skills: "Who said that to whom?" "What was said instead?" Classifications.	Partly located skills of detail finding and classifications.	Fully located details in the following skills: Who said that to whom? What was said instead? Classifications.
Identifying the main idea	Did not identify the sentence that holds a wealth of keywords, which is the main-idea sentence.	Partly identified keywords but did not identify the main-idea sentence.	Identified key sentences that have keywords, which are main-idea sentences.
Mapping of concepts (flow charts, Diffuse Mapping, Venn Diagrams)	Did not embed keywords and key sentences correctly in the three types of mappings: flow charts, Venn Diagrams and Diffuse Mapping.	Partly embedded keywords and key sentences in the three types of mappings: flow charts, Venn Diagrams and Diffuse Mapping.	Embedded keywords correctly and key sentences correctly in the three types of mappings: flow charts, Venn Diagrams and Diffuse Mapping.

Alternative Assessment:
Indicator of Reading and Comprehension on Three Levels of Thinking

Student name: _____ Class: _____ School: _____ Level of implementation: _____

Literal understanding	Starting out	Progress achieving a goal	Achieving the goal
Dividing into segments of meaning	Did not divide text according to correct segments of meaning, and were not cognizant of naming each paragraph.	Divided the text into meaning segments but did not name them.	Divided the text correctly into segments of meaning, and named each segment appropriately.
Locating of key sentences	Did not locate key sentences by using WH-words such as: Who is the segment talking about? What is the segment talking about?	Partly located key sentences by raising questions that separate the wheat from the chaff.	Located key sentences by questions such as who is the segment talking about? What is the segment talking about.
Locating of keywords	Did not locate keywords and separate the wheat from the chaff by asking WH-questions such as: Who is the segment talking about? What is the segment talking about?	Partly located keywords in key sentences and partly separated the wheat from the chaff by asking WH-questions such as: Who is the segment talking about? What is the segment talking about?	Located key words in key sentences and separated the wheat from the chaff by raising these questions.
Raising and classifying of questions	Did not use all WH-words in all three levels of thinking and did not classify them according to different classifications (5 classification tables).	Partly used WH-words in all three levels of thinking and partly classified them according to different classifications (5 classification tables).	Used all WH-words in all three levels of thinking and classified them according to different classifications (5 classification tables).
Summarization skills	Did not implement summarization skills by using keywords, key sentences and conjunctions.	Partly implemented summarization skills by using keywords, key sentences and conjunctions.	Fully implemented summarization skills by using keywords, key sentences and conjunctions.
Language enrichment	Did not implement the various linguistic assignments.	Partly implemented the various linguistic assignments.	Fully implemented the various linguistic assignments.

Alternative Assessment:
Indicator of Reading and Comprehension on Three Levels of Thinking

Student name: _____ Class: _____ School: _____ Level of implementation: _____

Literal understanding	Starting out	Progress achieving the goal	Achieving the goal
Drawing conclusions	Did not know how to draw conclusions from the text and implement conclusion-related assignments. Did not know how to raise main-idea, interpretive understanding questions.	Partly achieved the skill of drawing conclusions and partly implemented the interpretive understanding of main idea questions.	Could fully draw conclusions from the text and raise the correct questions about the main idea by using interpretive understanding.
Not-stated implicit main idea of the text	Did not know how to raise main-idea, interpretive-understanding questions and thus did not identify not-stated main idea.	Partly achieved the skill of raising questions and interpretive-understanding questions to identify not-stated main idea.	Fully achieved all skills needed for identifying not-stated main idea by using interpretive understanding questions.
Prediction of events	Did not know how to foretell the story's next event because of lack of understanding of its first part.	Partly knew to foretell the story's forthcoming events by leaning on the partial understanding of the story.	Full capacity of prediction forthcoming events of the story by relying on his/her understanding of the story.
Author's attitude	Did not know to identify the author's attitude by relying on the text and using interpretive understanding skills.	Partly identified the author's attitude through using interpretive understanding skills.	Fully understood author's attitude.

Alternative Assessment:
Indicator of Reading and Comprehension on Three Levels of Thinking

Student name: _____ Class: _____ School: _____ Level of implementation: _____

Literal understanding	Starting out	Progress achieving the goal	Achieving the goal
Distinguishing between fact and opinion	Did not identify the differences between facts and opinions and did not use identification skills for distinguishing between them.	Partly identified the differences between facts and opinions and partly used identification skills for distinguishing between them.	Identified the differences between facts and opinions and used good identification skills for distinguishing between them.
Form an Opinion	Did not know how to crystallize and formalize personal opinion while basing it on text.	Partly knew how to crystallize and formalize personal opinion while basing it on text.	Fully crystallized and formalized personal opinions that were an outcome of the text.
Solving of applied problems based on text	Could not apply his/her textual acquired knowledge to everyday life.	Could partly apply his/her textual acquired knowledge to everyday life.	Knew how to solve applied problems based on textual understanding and could accommodate it to his/her everyday life.

Learning Journal

Student name: _____ Class: _____

School: _____ Level of implementation: _____

🍃 Alternative Assessments

1. What does sequence mean?

   _____
   _____
   _____

2. Why is a narrative sequence so important in the story?

   _____
   _____
   _____

3. What have you learned about your learning process during this activity?

   _____
   _____
   _____

4. Why is it important to locate key words and sentences in the text?

   _____
   _____
   _____

5. With which WH-words did you locate keywords in the key sentences?

6. Which tools are there for locating a main idea?

7. Did you have any difficulty with locating the main idea?

8. What are raising and classifying questions important for?

9. What did you learn about yourself during this activity?

10. Why is it important to implement all the various phases of the assignment?

11. How would you be able to apply all the phases to other assignments as well?

12. Why do we need to locate textual details?

13. What is a flow chart and what it is used for?

14. Which skills did you use to build a flow chart?

15. You have been exposed to various types of mappings. When would you use each one of them?

___

16. Does the mapping system apply to your learning skills? If yes, explain why.

___

17. What have you learned about yourself through mapping?

___

18. Which kind of tools helped you draw your conclusions?

___

19. What kinds of clues belong to explicit content clues?

___

20. What types of clues belong to implicit content clues?

21. What can you learn from locating explicit and implicit content clues?

22. What do you think are the differences between the verbal, interpretive and implemental levels of understanding?

23. What did you find helpful and applicable for the assignments at the three levels of understanding?

24. Which of the three levels of thinking is more feasible to use?

25. Which of the three levels of thinking is more difficult to use?

26. How would you explain the notion of implemental level?

27. What is needed for completing the implemental level of assignments?

28. Which strategy would you change if you were to write it yourself?

29. Which type of skill did you like best and why?

Tables of Graded Language Patterns

Linguistic constructs	Samples	Important notes
Phase A: 1. Linguistic patterns Simple sentence– Nominal clause	* a yellow flower. * a table.	Nominal clauses are quite rare in English when the copula *be is omitted.
2. Simple sentence–verbal clause	* Uri stud**ies**. * Hanna sits.	It is recommended to begin with present simple and then move to past simple and present perfect.
3. Simple sentence + temporal clause	* Ronny studies **in the mornings.**	Temporal clauses are time complements that denote time like morning, afternoon, night, etc.
4. Simple sentence + locative clause	* The book is **on the table.**	Usually this linguistic construct consists of the sequence *verb + preposition. Prepositions are particles like on, under, off, next to, behind–words that could not be in plural voice.
5. Simple interrogative questions	* **Who** ate the cream? * **How** many pages are in the book? * **Where** do you live?	WH interrogatives can be identified by their WH-words such as why, where, who, when, whom, whether, etc.
6. Object clause	* I bought **the book.**	Usually an object clause will come after the verb and sometimes it is preceded by delimitative ***the.**
7. Possessive clause	* I **have** the book. * I **don't have** the book.	Usually these are marked by the word *have.

Tables of Graded Language Patterns

Linguistic constructs	Samples	Important notes
8. Auxiliary verbs + verbs Can, could, shall, should, will, would, may, might, have, had, etc.	* I **must learn** Hebrew. * I **can learn** Hebrew.	Auxiliary verbs (or help-words) provide an emotive force to the sentence and verbs in this construct will stay uninflected. They should be taught after teaching simple past and present.
9. Causal clause	* We did not go on the trip **because** it was raining. * We went to eat **since** we were hungry.	Causal clauses may be identified by causal words such as **because, since, as, for, therefore,** etc., which usually head an independent clause. However, their position might be at the beginning or end of sentence.
10. Result constructs	* The ox could tolerate no more of this work, **so** he asked the man.	Using conjunctions like *as a result, therefore, so, hence* that denote the construct of result.
11. Comparative clause	* Ronny plods **like** a turtle.	Through using comparative words such as **like, as, such that, such as,** etc., two facts are being compared to each other. Usually, a comparative clause will come at the end of sentence.

Tables of Graded Language Patterns

Linguistic constructs	Samples	Important notes
12. Contrast clause but, on one hand...., on the other hand, in contrast, contrastingly	* Danny runs fast. Hanna, **on the other hand**, runs faster.	Contrast is achieved through using contrast words such as but etc. The construct consists of two facts that are compared and contrasted to each other.
13. Adverbial clause	* answered the wife **laughing.**	An independent clause that describes the modus in which the verb occurred: she answered while she was laughing.
14. Final clause	* They went to sleep late **for** they wanted to watch the match.	Usually are identifiable by words such as **for, aiming at, targeting.**

Tables of Graded Language Patterns

Linguistic constructs	Samples	Important notes
Phase B: 15. Direct speech, Indirect speech	* Mom told Tali, **"Picking mushrooms in the forest is forbidden."** * Mom told Tali **that** it is forbidden to pick mushrooms in the forest.	Direct speech construct is marked by the use of quotation marks and a comma that precedes it. Indirect construct is marked by the use of subordinating words such as **that, which, WH-words and more.**
16. Idioms	* Keep an eye on… Actions speak louder than words. * Leave you in the dust.	An idiom is a phrase or combination of words that their conclusive meaning is bigger than the separate meaning of each word on its own. There is an added value to the idiom. Usually the words are connected in a firm unchangeable way.
17. In order for + will (future)	* **In order** for you **to** achieve high grades in your exams, you must prepare for them.	In the construct "in order for" when it is used as a conditional phrase use auxiliary verbs like "must", "should" etc.
18. Conditional sentence	* If you had studied harder you would have succeeded.	**Would** in the protasis, the dependent clause that describes the condition; **will** in the apodosis, the independent clause that describes the consequences.
19. Comparatives–more, -er (nic**er**), less, as	* Ronny is smart**er than** I in math. * The new employee is **less** professional than the rest of us. * Daniel is **as** clever **as** his grandfather.	Comparatives usually set a comparison between two elements, usually by the use of *more, -er* (nicer) + **than**. In the construct *as… as* the idea of comparison is transferred without using than.

Tables of Graded Language Patterns

Linguistic constructs	Samples	Important notes
20. Superlative forms– Most + a superlative adjective Adjective + est Best, most	* The new movie is the **most successful** movie this summer. * It is the **funniest** movie I have ever seen.	Adjectives that are being used to convey an exaggeration.
21. Copulas	* Dogs are pets. * A tiger is a wild animal.	A copula links a subjective clause to the complement usually by using the verb *be* (is, are, was, were). The complement can be either a nominative, an adjectival or propositional clause.
22. Yes/no questions	* "Did you beat me?" yelled the hare to the tortoise.	A question whose answer can be either yes or no.
23. Either... or Neither... nor	* You can **either** run fast **or** try even harder but you're **neither** going to beat me **nor** are you going to win the victory cup.	**Either...or** is a pronoun and adverb signifying two possibilities. **Neither... nor** signifies the absence of both possibilities.

Table of Workbook 1 Texts and Skills

Skills \ Texts	The Tortoise and the Hare	Why Are the Leaves of the Tree Blue?	Why Does the Ox Walk Slowly?	A Nice Tale that Happened in our Town	The Sweetest Music in the World	Keep an Eye on the Door
Literal understanding						
Sequence	*	*	*		*	*
Locating details	*	*	*			*
Main idea	*	*		*	*	
Separating the wheat from the chaff	*	*	*		*	*
Mapping of concepts			*		*	
Raising and classifying questions	*				*	
Classifications (classification tables)	*		*			
Summarization			*			
Interpretive understanding						
Locating an implicit not-stated main idea		*	*	*		
Prediction of events	*	*	*			
Identifying the author's attitude	*					
Drawing conclusions and analyzing characters			*	*		
Implementation						
Distinguishing between opinions and facts	*					
Problem solving	*	*	*			
Language enrichment	*					
Alternative assessment						
Learning journal	*	*	*	*	*	*
Indicator	*	*	*	*	*	*

www.ingramcontent.com/pod-product-compliance
Lightning Source LLC
Chambersburg PA
CBHW042031150426
43200CB00002B/17